stump

written by Jeff Hendley

illustrated by Tess Hendley

13 ISBN: 978-1-935256-34-2

Published by L'Edge Press
L'Edge Press
PO Box 1652
Boone, NC 28607

STUMP.
You are the most REAL person I know.
When I grow up — I want to be just like you.

FOREWORD

I wanted to write a story about one of my heroes. His nickname is Stump—one of my brothers. Stump is eleven months younger than me. We are the same age for 33 days each year. When I think about Stump, this story is what comes to mind. It is how I see Stump and the impact he has on the world around him.

Awhile back I asked one of our nieces to illustrate this story. Tess, thanks for letting God use you to tell this story.

Mark—Stump—thank you for encouraging me to walk with God everyday.

Tess Hendley is a creative 10 year old that is passionate about art and creative writing. She has a brother that drives her crazy but loves him anyway. And her biggest fans are her mother and father.

stump

"Tell us the story about Stump," yelled the little saplings.

The young, growing treelings had all gathered in the open field. It was getting late in the day and after all the festivities it was time for Tree Stories.

The eldest of the trees — the Great Willows, the Grand Oaks — would stir the imaginations of the young treelings with stories of trees gone by.

"Don't you want to hear a story about the Mighty Oaks or the Soaring Pines or the One Tree," the elder tree asked.

"No," cried all the saplings. "We want to hear the story of Stump."

With a great sigh and a smile of joy, the eldest of all the trees began the Tale of Stump.

The first indication that all was not well with a particular young tree came from the early comments of the other saplings:

"What kind of tree are you?"

"We've never seen a tree like you before."

As the other young trees formed, developed, and grew it was easy to tell what kind of tree they would grow into. It was not hard to see whether a tree would be strong, sturdy or weak. But one particular tree did not grow like the rest of the saplings. It was hard to tell what kind of tree it was going to be. Was this one of the rare trees that the Great TreeShepherd had brought into the forest? No one knew.

It was not long before the other trees named this odd tree. Youngsters everywhere loved to give nicknames to each other. Names like Tower, Stretch, Hairy, and Shiny were some of the names given that matched these young trees. This odd tree did not look like the other young trees. This odd tree was a short tree. And time did not increase its stature. Short and stocky. Thick and burly. Soon, the name of "Stump" took root among the treelings and thus, Stump it was.

Some of the treelings even called him "Stump — the Strong." Short and stocky but powerful he was. Stronger than an oak. Stump early on in his ageless life would stand and protect the other treelings from danger. Stump was always the winner in the treestling matches (wrestling matches among the treelings).

As the years passed, Stump grew — a little. Small in stature but strong. Every tree in the forest had something special that the Great TreeShepherd had seen fit to graft into the tree. And Stump was no different. Stump's specialness was in his strength. And time would only tell how this strength would be seen and used.

As time continued to spend itself, Stump came to live on the edge of the forest, away from the other trees. He chose to live at the entrance of the forest. Here Stump could see and know the wonders, the beauty, and the ugliness of the world.

Stump drew apart from the other trees and planted his roots by the great stream that wound its way at the entrance of the forest. Why did he choose to live at the entrance to the forest, away from the deep shade and comfort of the Inner Forest? No one knew. But Stump wanted to live around all the creatures of the world and the forest. He wanted to live and be a part of all life not just the life of the forest. Here he lived. And here his strength continued to grow. Fed by the Great Stream that flowed past the forest.

The storms of life were harsher here. Stump was battered by the weather, the hot and cold of the seasons, the harshness of the life lived by all who chose to live apart from the forest. But here, he came to know the other creatures of the world. These creatures were drawn to Stump. For in Stump they saw something that made them want to stop and rest. They saw the battered tree.

These creatures came to Stump to live in his branches, rest in his shade and share in his quiet strength. Creatures who feared living things would come and settle in his thick branches and leaves. The shade was so thick that it was cooler than other places below the leaves. Often creatures would make their home in the rough and broken bark of this strong tree.

Life had caused Stump to suffer. But in his suffering life was given to others. Stump had grown so strong that no storm, wind, force of nature or disease could cause him to bend or bring harm to the creatures who came to this tree for shelter.

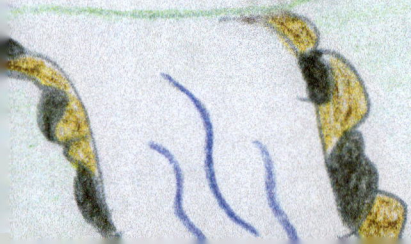

Stump was different. His outer shell made up of sap and bark was battered and had caught the harshest diseases of the world. He seemed ever shorter as time marched on. Stump grew weary of all the ugliness and the pain of the diseases.

But still he stood rooted there by this great stream. To look upon this tree was to feel a great sadness. To gaze upon him was to see the ugly scars of life and to know that the sufferings of life had not passed this special tree. But in this diseased and battered shell, the creatures of the world found comfort. For they knew that if they could share time with this special tree they too could find the strength to withstand anything life had to bring to them. So, Stump became a place where any creature who needed strength and rest could come.

Stump knew pain. He knew he was battered and bruised. At times Stump wished the great TreeShepherd would come and take him to the Great Forest — away from all this pain and suffering. But Stump was glad he could give shelter to the creatures. He was pleased that his shade gave rest to those who sought it. He was glad to be alive and he grew proud of his name — The Stump.

One day a stirring could be heard throughout the forest. A whisper of wind. The song being sung by the trees spoke of the coming of the Great TreeShepherd. Occasionally, the TreeShepherd would come and visit the forests of the world. It was a rare event. The forest where Stump lived had never known a visit from the Great TreeShepherd. But He was coming. The stories told that when He came He came looking for that one special tree.

Soon, the TreeShepherd appeared. He glided through the trees. A great hush fell over the forest. The TreeShepherd came and stood before Stump. Surprised — Stump looked up and saw the Great TreeShepherd smiling at him.

Stump could only stare. The TreeShepherd spoke. His voice was like the richness of the earth and as quiet as the clouds.

"Stump", he said. "I am glad you have done well, my special tree. You have done all that I expected of you."

Stump looked bewildered.

Stump asked, "What do you mean?"

The TreeShepherd spoke to Stump in a way that the whole forest could hear.

"I chose you to be different. I placed you here. I chose you to bear the pain and the disease of the world. I chose you to stand-alone here by this stream, in your battered and scarred life so you could provide shelter and rest to those who needed it."

"I wanted you to give welcome and shelter to all my creatures — I wanted them to see Me in you."

Then the Great TreeShepherd let the mist and the clouds clear away and there He stood, the Great TreeShepherd.

Scarred. Broken. Battered. Short.

A stump of a tree.

The TreeShepherd said to Stump, "I chose you to be like me so that all the creatures and trees would know me as I really am. Thank you, Stump, for letting me live through you. It has been hard for you and I thank you. Stump — the Strong, I want you to continue to root here by the Great Stream. The waters from the Stream flow from the Great Forest. These waters will refresh you and all the others. These waters will keep you strong. I want you to continue to give shelter, rest and safety to all those who seek them."

With these final words, the Great TreeShepherd departed.

The elder tree looked down upon the young treelings and saw the light dancing from their dew-laden faces. The wondrous look each face held revealed the inner most desires of each treeling. These young trees wanted to do what Stump had done. Each beginning tree wanted to be a special tree.

The wise elder tree then spoke to the heart of each treeling. "You are a Special Tree. Each of you. The Great TreeShepherd wants you to be special and live like you are special. Like Stump — The Strong, you can also be strong. Use your strength for others. Drink deeply from the Great Stream. And the Great TreeShepherd will live in and through you...just like He lived in and through Stump."

Blessed are those who trust in the Lord...
They are like trees planted along a riverbank, with roots
that reach deep into the water. Such trees are not
bothered by the heat or worried by long months of
drought. Their leaves stay green, and they go
right on producing delicious fruit.

Jeremiah 17:7 NLT

www.ingramcontent.com/pod-product-compliance
Lightning Source LLC
LaVergne TN
LVHW080248090426
835508LV00042BA/1495